Franklin Watts

First published in Great Britain in 2016 by The Watts Publishing Group

From the TV series *What's the Big Idea?* directed by Tanguy de Kermel,
© 2013 / 2014 Planet Nemo Animation / Skyline Entertainment / Motion Magic /
La Planète Rouge / Señalcolombia / Educar / Xilam Animation, loosely based
on the original work *Le livre des grands contraires philosophiques,* written by
Oscar Brenifier and illustrated by Jacques Després, pubished by Éditions Nathan.
Images taken from the Philozidées series, by the same authors from the same publisher.
Original script by Alan Gilbey.
First published in French as *Pourquoi je suis jaloux?*

Copyright © Éditions Nathan - Paris, France 2014

Translation © Franklin Watts 2016
English text and adaptation by Elise Short

Series Editor: Elise Short
Series Advisor: Jackie Hamley
Design: Peter Scoulding and Cathryn Gilbert

Dewey number 152.4'8
HB ISBN 978 1 4451 4723 9

Printed in China

Franklin Watts
An imprint of
Hachette Children's Group
Part of The Watts Publishing Group
Carmelite House
50 Victoria Embankment
London EC4Y 0DZ

An Hachette UK Company

www.hachette.co.uk

www.franklinwatts.co.uk

FSC www.fsc.org

MIX
Paper from
responsible sources
FSC® C104740

Why am I jealous?

W
FRANKLIN WATTS
LONDON•SYDNEY

It's playtime. Hugo rushes to meet his friends to play yoyo. But Sam and Little Ballerina don't even notice him. They are too busy playing with other children.

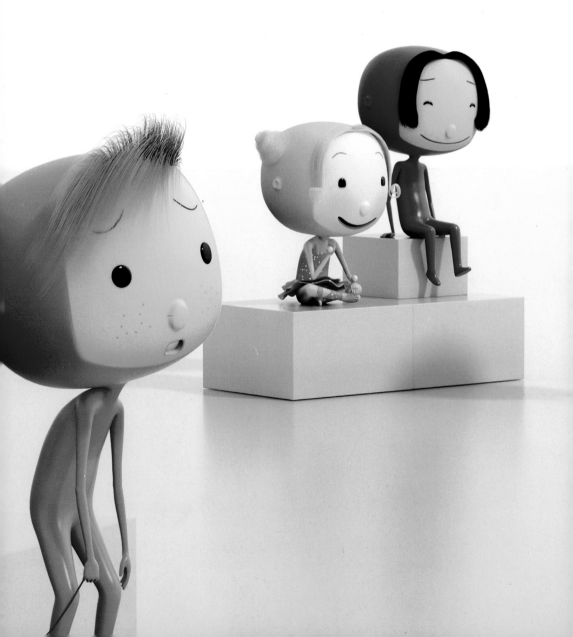

Hugo feels both cross and sad.
What a strange feeling! **Could he be jealous?**

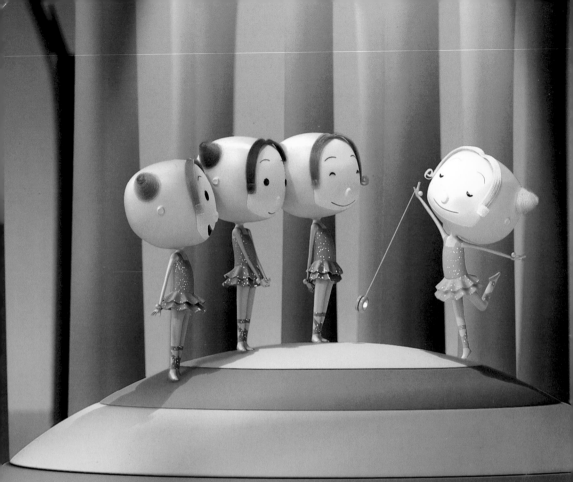

Yeti feels all alone, too. He has spotted Little Ballerina showing her friends yoyo tricks and all of a sudden he feels left out.

What if she never wants to play with him ever again?

Just like Hugo, he starts feeling jealous.

Now Hugo is really angry.

"Why are they all so obsessed with their stupid yoyos? I want my friends to play with me!"

What's happened to Hugo? When he's jealous, he's not the nice boy we know...

Someone else is feeling jealous: Hugo's friend Lucas has got a new little sister and he doesn't feel important any more. He thinks his mummy only cares about her now.

But Lucas thinks hard. "No, that can't be right," he tells himself. "Mummy still loves me just as much, it's just that jealousy is giving me the wrong idea."

Back in the forest, Yeti has found a way to attract the Little Ballerina's attention; he is teaching her new yoyo tricks!

Now it's her other friends' turn to be jealous.
"Just because he has a yoyo and we haven't!" one of them cries.

"It's not fair!"

Hugo is still sulking.

"I don't care who my friends play with! I'm not angry at all and I'm not sad either. No way!"

Really? But it seems like he's still in a very bad mood...

Honestly, being jealous isn't any fun at all!

Is there a way to stop feeling jealous?

how exciting! The roller coaster at the forest funfair is now open.

"**Roll up, roll up** children, take your seats!" calls the Ringmaster.

Yeti and Little Ballerina jump into the first bumper car and start going round and round and round! They can't seem to stop...

Behind them, green with envy, Little Ballerina's friends are in hot pursuit.

"She doesn't like us anymore, so let's bump into her!"

Brrrroom!

Here comes Hugo.

"What are you waiting for, my boy? Go and join them!" the Ringmaster whispers to him.

Hugo is thinking, he'd like to join them in their jealous race but he hesitates.

"Maybe, the best way to **stop feeling bad feelings** is to not let them take you for a ride..."

"Hey Hugo, see what I can do with my yoyo! Do you want me to teach you?"

"Yes please!"
cries Hugo,
very happy to
have his friend
back at last.

The ride is over now for Yeti, Little Ballerina and her friends.

What a surprise! They are all very pleased to see each other again!

All this chasing around was a lot of fun after all!

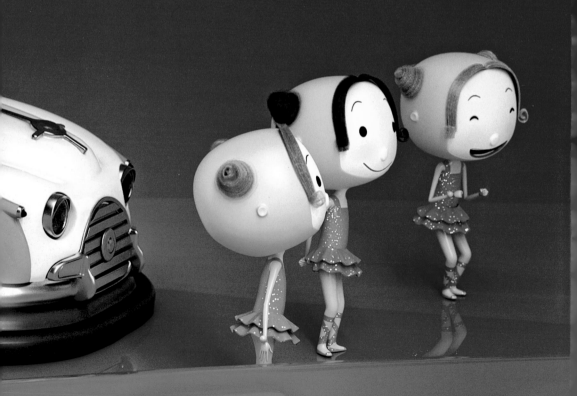

"Oh I really missed you guys!" says Little Ballerina. "It's a lot more fun when we all play together, don't you think?"

Yeti jumps for joy!

Hugo understands now; **to get rid of jealousy** there's nothing like moving on and having a good time with a friend.

"For example, learning new yoyo tricks or joining in to play together are perfect ways to forget all about those bad feelings," laughs Hugo.

What do you think?

A note about sharing this book

The *What's the Big Idea?* series has been developed to provide a starting point for introducing philosophy to young children. It aims to promote thinking skills in its readers, developing their questioning of the world around them and encouraging them to make up their own mind about ideas and abstract concepts.

Why Am I Jealous?

This story explores the effects of jealousy and the situations in which it arises. It also encourages children to think about what jealousy is and ways to stop feeling jealous.

After reading the book, talk about it with your child or class:

• What was the story about? Why did Hugo/Yeti/Lucas feel jealous and left out? Have the children ever felt jealous about someone or something and felt left out? Encourage the children to draw on their own experience.

• How did the characters react to feeling left out? How did they feel?

• How do you know you're feeling jealous?

• Jealousy can make you feel all kinds of other feelings. Which ones

do Hugo and his friends feel? Are there any others?

• Can we choose whether or not to feel jealous? Or can we only choose whether or not to act on our feelings of jealousy?

• Is there anything good about feeling jealous? Ask the children to justify their answer with examples.